For more books by Katrina Liu visit
www.lycheepress.com

ISBN 978-1-953281-70-8

Copyright © 2022 by Katrina Liu. All rights reserved. No part of this book may be reproduced, transmitted, or stored in an information retrieval system in any form or by any means, graphic, electronic, or mechanical, including photocopying, taping, and recording, without prior written permission from the publisher. First edition 2022. Licensed clip art by Donnay Style.

SQUEEZE the day!

Share your sweet dedications

Made in the USA
Coppell, TX
16 June 2023